MORMONS

History · Culture · Beliefs

Answers to Commonly Asked Questions About
The Church of Jesus Christ of Latter-day Saints

Mormons: History, Culture, Beliefs
copyright 2005
White Horse Books
1347 S. Glenmare St.
Salt Lake City, UT 84105
and Pat Bagley
all rights reserved
Printed in the United States

First Edition

9 8 7 6 5 4 3 2 1

ISBN 0-9744860-3-5

editor: Dan Thomas

Acknowledgements. Shane Asbridge, Suzie Berseau, Alec Bagley,
the Durham family, Tamara England, Gerald Ericksen, Kent Frogley,
Brooke Johnson, Christy Karras, LDS Church Archives, Oliver Lewis,
Margaret Reiser, *The Salt Lake Tribune*, Peggy Stack, Utah
Historical Society, Meg Vinton.

MORMONS
History • Culture • Beliefs

Answers to Commonly Asked Questions About
The Church of Jesus Christ of Latter-day Saints

Salt Lake City

GLOSSARY

Apostle — Highest office of the priesthood, usually referring to a member of the Twelve

Bishop — Unpaid clergyman of a congregation (ward), similar to a pastor, priest, or rabbi

Elder — Title used to address a holder of the higher priesthood, a general authority, or a male missionary

Family Home Evening — Usually held on Mondays, families gather for activities that promote togetherness

Fast Sunday — Members fast for two meals and donate equivalent cost to assist the poor and disadvantaged

Firesides — Informal gatherings, usually in homes or wards, featuring a speaker or program on a religious theme

First Presidency — The president of the church and his two counselors; highest ranking body in the church

Garments — White undergarments worn by members who have received their temple endowments

General Authority — Title used to address members of the First Presidency, the Twelve, the Seventy, and Presiding Bishopric

General Conference — Churchwide semi-annual assembly; held every April and October in Salt Lake City

Investigator — A prospective convert to the church who is receiving missionary instruction

Jack Mormon — A lapsed Mormon; usually referring to one who smokes or drinks alcohol

Mutual — A weekly youth activities meeting for teenagers, usually held at a ward

Priesthood — Authority given to men to act in God's name; includes Aaronic (lesser) and Melchizedek (higher)

Primary — Religious education and activities for children ages 3 to 11

Quorum of the Twelve Apostles — "The Twelve;" assists the First Presidency; second highest quorum of the church

Quorum of the Seventy — "The Seventy;" assists the Twelve; currently there are five Quorums of the Seventy

Relief Society — The church's official organization for adult women

Restoration — The re-establishment of the Gospel of Jesus Christ through Joseph Smith

Returned Missionary — One who has completed his or her mission

Stake — A geographical, ecclesiastical subdivision, composed of several wards; similar to a diocese in the Catholic Church

Testimony — A personal belief about the truth of the doctrine and mission of the church

Tithing — "Tenth;" a law that asks 10% of one's income

Ward — The basic ecclesiastical unit of the church, consisting of 300-500 members, presided over by a bishop

Word of Wisdom — Revealed by God in 1833, this code of health forbids alcohol, tobacco, illegal drugs, tea and coffee

Zion — The geographic location where righteous followers gather to live by the Gospel

For an expanded glossary, visit www.lds.org/newsroom/glossary

TABLE OF CONTENTS

Mormonism, because it has maintained itself, must be reckoned with. Unorthodox as much of its theological and social experimentation has been, it never lost its hold on the things of this earth. In the midst of the most incredible theological labyrinths, it has always been at bottom, among the people, a practical religion.

—Wallace Stegner
Mormon Country

CONCERNING MORMONS

Mormonism is a wholly original, American-born faith. Its prophets attest that it is a restoration of Jesus Christ's ancient church. It has intrigued scholars with its doctrine, puzzled critics with its success, and inspired millions with its message. In 175 years, it has grown from 6 men meeting in a log cabin to a worldwide movement of 12 million.

Mormons are known as a hard-working, politically conservative people with strong ties to family and respect for authority. They avoid some things like sin because these things *are* sins in their religion: alcohol, tobacco, coffee and swearing, for instance. Mormons suffer lower rates of cancer than any other group in America and are famously upbeat about the power of their faith to promote a happy, healthy and meaningful life.

Mormons are members of The Church of Jesus Christ of Latter-day Saints, or LDS. The term "Mormon" was originally applied to the followers of Joseph Smith by his detractors. It was a mocking reference to the "golden book" that Smith translated into the Book of Mormon. Quite quickly, the people who believed that Smith was a prophet of God co-opted the term and proudly called themselves "Mormons." However, if the point is to blend in, don't ask, "Are you a Mormon?" Instead, folks in the know say, "Are you LDS?" Don't bother asking why, that's one question this book doesn't answer.

It should be acknowledged that the church discourages the use of "Mormon," in favor of "members of the Church of Jesus Christ," to emphasize their Christian roots. But the rank and file still happily use the handier term, "Mormon," to identify themselves. It is also the name used in this book.

Impressions about Mormons are often hilariously off the mark. Some think Mormons wear beards, black frock coats, and drive buggies chock-full of polygamous wives. In the South at the turn of the 20th century, ministers preached over the pulpit that Mormons had horns and tails, just like the Devil. Of course Mormons aren't demonic, but they can be devilishly clumsy about dispelling myths and stereotypes. They take pride in being "a peculiar people," as God calls His chosen in the Old Testament. Their exotic distinctiveness is a badge of honor.

In fact, Mormons are not that peculiar. They struggle in their marriages, battle rebellious teenagers, fall ill, endure tragedy and suffer doubt, just like the rest of the world. However, there *is* a peculiar attitude, fueled by their beliefs, that brings a fundamental hopefulness and meaning to all these experiences.

It is a faith that has managed to remain relevant, even as it hurtles full-throttle into the 21st century. Some even say that Mormonism is on the brink of becoming a major world religion. So what do Mormons believe? What is their daily life like? Do they have more than one wife? And if not, then how did they get associated with such an outlandish notion? These are all common questions that deserve straightforward answers.

A lot has been written about Mormonism, most of it with an agenda. Some of the most active religious sites on the internet are dedicated to defending or debunking Mormon tenets and teachings. This book recognizes the volatility of its subject, but endeavors to look at Mormonism on its own terms, sticking to the facts. This is not a publication of the LDS Church, nor is it beholden to the church's critics. It has no agenda but to inform through words and pictures.

BEGINNINGS
How Did Mormonism Start?

Joseph Smith was born on the American frontier in 1805. As a young man he was exposed to the religious fervor sweeping upstate New York—various churches and Christian movements were contending with each other for followers, all claiming to be the "true path" to God.

In the spring of 1820, the 14-year-old Joseph was concerned about the state of his own soul. He decided to pray for guidance. By his own account, he was answered with a visitation from God and Jesus Christ.

This was the "First Vision"—the beginning of Joseph Smith's prophetic calling. Over the following years he would receive instruction from a number of angelic visitors. Various Old and New Testament personalities appeared to the young American seer—such as Elijah and Paul—as did previously unknown prophets from ancient America. It was one of these, the Angel Moroni, who entrusted Smith with a history of the ancestors of the American Indians, written on gold plates. Smith's translation, called the Book of Mormon, would be the corner-stone of the new religion (see p. 14).

In 1830, Smith officially organized his new church. Its stated purpose was to restore all the gifts and offices that Jesus had endowed in His early church. Smith taught that the church Jesus organized in Judea had, over the centuries, fallen away from the truth and into apostasy. The new church of latter-day saints would be a restoration of God's one true church.

PFB

"The First Vision." God the Father and Jesus Christ instruct the 14-year-old Joseph Smith not to join any of the churches of his time, as they were all in error.

Not everyone was happy with the idea of a new Christianity. To avoid growing persecution in New York, the church moved to Ohio, then Missouri, and finally Illinois. Smith and his followers always seemed just one step ahead of angry mobs. In Missouri, the Mormon experience was especially cruel. Governor Lilburn Boggs issued an "extermination order" which proclaimed, "The Mormons must be treated as enemies, and must be exterminated or driven from the state, if necessary, for the public good." Three days later, 17 Mormons were killed by the Missouri militia and their bodies were dumped in a well. The tragedy has become known as the Haun's Mill Massacre.

WHAT'S IN A NAME?

Even Mormons are surprised to learn that the name of their church hasn't always been the same. When organized in 1830, it was simply called The Church of Christ. In an 1834 conference, it was changed to The Church of Latter-day Saints. The name was finally settled by an 1838 revelation which mandated The Church of Jesus Christ of Latter-day Saints. The name conveys that it is a modern restoration of the same church Christ established among His saints 2000 years ago.

PFB

Joseph Smith and his brother, Hyrum, were assassinated by a mob while awaiting trial in Carthage, Illinois.

Fleeing the state in the dead of winter, more than 10,000 destitute Mormons regrouped in Illinois at a bend of the Mississippi River. Initially welcomed by the people of Illinois, the Mormons proceeded to build a city unique in the annals of American history. They called it Nauvoo (see box, below). Joseph Smith was Mayor of Nauvoo, Commanding General of the Nauvoo Legion, as well as leader of the Mormon Church.

Even while Nauvoo prospered and grew, rumors of disturbing religious practices followed the Mormons to Illinois. Some neighbors felt threatened by the growing political power of the Mormons, who ignored national parties and voted as a block. A warrant was issued for Smith's arrest when *The Nauvoo Expositor,* a newspaper critical of the Mormon prophet, was destroyed on his orders. On June 27, 1844, while awaiting trial, Joseph Smith was murdered by a mob that stormed his jail cell.

Various pretenders aspired to lead the bereft church. There was no clear successor and persecution from outside was growing. Enemies of the church were confident they were seeing the last of the Mormons.

For more Mormon history, visit **www.lds.org/churchhistory**.

By most accounts, Joseph Smith was a dynamic personality. Tall for his time (6'1"), contemporaries often mention his piercing blue eyes and engaging manner. Mormon folklore mentions a fondness for physical tests of strength, such as wrestling and "stick pulling." Stick pulling was a frontier favorite in which opponents, seated sole to sole, gripped a stick. The winner managed to pull his opponent up and over. In the Mormon telling, Smith never lost.

NAUVOO

Nauvoo was built up from a malarial swamp on a bend of the Mississippi River. Joseph Smith named the city from the Hebrew word for "beautiful." It would be the headquarters of the church from 1839 to 1846, becoming the richest and most powerful city of the American interior, even larger than Chicago. At its height, it boasted a population of 16,000.

The Illinois legislature granted Smith and the Mormons a charter that allowed them their own courts, police, and even a militia: The Nauvoo Legion. While this arrangement suited Smith and his followers, it created explosive resentment among those who were at odds with Mormon aims.

Dissension within the church and growing hostility from the state of Illinois doomed Nauvoo. In February 1846, the Mormons left as they had come— refugees from persecution. The abandoned temple fell victim to arsonists and a tornado. Its blocks were used for building material by the French emigrants who later settled the town.

In 2002, the Mormon Church rebuilt the temple on its original site. Today much of Mormon Nauvoo has been restored and is a popular tourist destination for Mormons (see p. 44). **www.nauvoo.com.**

The Nauvoo Temple was the largest structure west of the Alleghenies. After its dedication, it only stood for two and a half years.

THE TREK WEST

Why is Utah Mormon?

Brigham Young took charge of a church teetering on the brink of disaster. The charismatic Smith had been murdered and various factions were openly vying for control. Away on a mission at the time of Smith's death, "Brother Brigham" hurried back and, as president of the Quorum of the Twelve Apostles (see p. 24), successfully asserted his right to lead the church.

Hostility to the Mormons in Illinois continued to grow, and Young realized there would be no rest as long as they lived among people who didn't share their beliefs. Smith had prophesied that his people would find refuge in the Rocky Mountains. Young could only rely on rumors of habitable lands, but he determined that Smith's vision of a home in the West was their best chance to escape persecution. In February, 1846, the Mormons loaded their wagons and crossed the frozen Mississippi, abandoning their homes in Nauvoo.

It was on the trek west that Young's genius manifested itself. He never claimed the extent of Smith's spiritual gifts, but what he had in buckets was a knack for organization and leadership. He marshalled the wagon trains along military lines and made provisions for those that would follow. Departing companies of pioneers planted crops for those coming later. It was a masterful retreat that trailblazed the way for thousands of converts who continued to arrive from the eastern United States, Britain and the Scandinavian countries.

On July 24, 1847, a vanguard of 143 men, 3 women, and 2 children entered the Valley of the Great Salt Lake. Years later it was remembered that Young, gazing out at the grassy valley, said, "This is the right place." July 24th is still celebrated in Utah as Pioneer Day, surpassing even the 4th of July in popularity.

Brigham Young has been called "The American Moses."

Utah Historical Society

"The Gathering to Zion" was preached as a duty of all church members. Converts were expected to emigrate to the Mormon home in the West. By wagons, handcarts, and later rail, nearly 100,000 made the trek. Even converts from Polynesia left their island homes to settle in the deserts of the Great Basin.

The early years of Mormon settlement were difficult and tenuous. Pioneers were plagued by pests (see box, opposite), drought and disease. Harvests in the second year were so paltry that they almost starved. But their fortunes changed dramatically with the discovery of gold at Sutter's Mill in California (coincidentally, most of the employees at the mill were Mormons on their way to Utah. Unbelievably, they packed up and left the richest gold strike in history when Young called them back).

Eager 49ers, taking the quickest overland route through Utah to the gold fields, bought Mormon wheat and livestock at premium prices. Over-burdened gold-seekers abandoned valuable goods, such as stoves and pianos, on the trail, much to the benefit of the locals. After a few trying years, the future of the Mormons in the West was assured.

Mormon settlement quickly expanded. Three years after their arrival, Brigham Young was appointed governor. Within twenty years, Mormon pioneers would establish over 300 communities in places as far-flung as California,

WAGONS HO!

The trek west was accomplished in wagons that were 4 feet wide, 10 feet long, and covered with canvas. Between 1847 and 1869 (the year of completion of the transcontinental railroad), nearly 70,000 Mormons moved west.

PFB

"The Bulletin of the Plains" was information written on buffalo skulls and left at the side of the trail for those who followed.

PFB

PFB

Wagons were expensive. An ingenious way for poor converts to cross the plains was suggested by Brigham Young—handcarts. Handcart pioneers generally made the crossing in good time, but two late-starting companies were stranded by blizzards. 213 died before being saved by rescue parties from Salt Lake City.

Canada and Mexico. They envisioned a vast kingdom that included most of the western U.S. They called it "Deseret," a Book of Mormon name meaning "honeybee."

The U.S. government had other plans. First, it made clear that the name of the territory would be "Utah," after the native Ute people. Then it proceeded to carve up Deseret. The states of Arizona, Nevada, and large parts of Colorado, Idaho, California and New Mexico all came from the Mormon kingdom in the West.

In 1852, Young deemed the church stable enough in its mountain stronghold to finally reveal to the world a doctrine that had been kept secret by Mormon leaders since Nauvoo. It was called "The New and Everlasting Covenant of Marriage" and had been claimed as a revelation from God by Joseph Smith. Smith's infuriated wife, Emma Hale, burned a transcription of the revelation when it was first shown to her. But Smith had made copies. Like the patriarchs of the Old Testament, it commanded righteous men to take multiple wives.

It was a call for polygamy.

The outrage that erupted in the nation and beyond once again put the Mormons and their church in dire peril. The turmoil would last for almost forty years, as Americans sought to stamp out this threat to traditional family values. Find out more at **www.history.utah.gov**.

The voracious "Mormon Cricket" (Anabrus Simplex) is actually a grasshopper. Some pioneers thought it so ugly they said it resembled a cross between a spider and a buffalo.

PFB

PFB

THE MIRACLE OF THE GULLS

In the spring of 1848, the pioneers planted their crops, anticipating a good harvest from the rich soil of the Salt Lake Valley. May and June brought drought, then swarms of crickets began devouring what was left of the parched stalks of wheat. In places, the bugs were so thick it seemed the ground itself was moving. For two weeks, men, women and children battled the bugs with shovels, sticks and brooms. Even burning and drowning didn't work. The exhausted settlers turned to prayer. Seagulls arrived from the Great Salt Lake, and for weeks gorged on crickets, saving the crops. Today a monument dedicated to the gulls stands in downtown Salt Lake City. Ironically, Utah's state bird is the California Gull.

P O L Y G A M Y

Do Mormons Have More Than One Wife?

Mormon polygamy continues to fascinate, much to the chagrin of the modern church, which disavowed the practice over a hundred years ago. Mormons today tend to view polygamy as a passing episode in which God tested the faith of His fledgling church. When the people successfully proved their devotion, the test was ended. The reality is a bit more complicated.

When Joseph Smith first confided to a chosen few that polygamy was to be revived, their initial reaction was shock and disgust. This new commandment tested the loyalty of Smith's followers, most of whom came of New England puritan roots. Typical was Brigham Young, who said he "desired the grave." Following serious soul-searching, most were persuaded that polygamy was a biblical commandment that God wanted restored. Young would eventually overcome his reluctance and marry over 40 women.

When first introduced, the practice was kept secret. Polygamy was tightly regulated, allowed only with the permission of church leaders. Often a man with means was encouraged— sometimes commanded—to take another wife to provide for her and her children.

A 19th century Mormon polygamist with his wives and children.

LDS Church Archives

As a matter of practice, women were free to refuse polygamist marriages. Divorces were liberally given to those who found polygamy too much of a trial. Even some of Young's wives sought and were granted divorces. However, the pressure to obey God's revealed truth meant a great many women felt trapped.

The 1852 disclosure of polygamy brought a worldwide outcry. In the United States, the platform of the brand-new Republican party called for the abolition of polygamy and slavery, "the twin relics of barbarism." Officials were sent from Washington with orders to assert federal control in the Utah Territory. They were generally ignored or subverted by the Mormons. When a federal judge was chased out of Utah (Mormons claimed with some

In *Roughing It*, **MARK TWAIN** tells of a visit to Salt Lake City. He confesses that he intended to launch a righteous crusade against polygamy, but upon seeing the local women, wrote, "The man that marries one of them has done an act of Christian charity . . . and the man that marries sixty of them has done a deed of open-handed generosity so sublime that the nations should stand uncovered in his presence and worship in silence."

WANTED!

In the 1880s, Congress cracked down hard on polygamous Utah. Hundreds of prominent Mormons were relentlessly tracked down and imprisoned. Leaders that evaded capture were forced to run the church while in hiding. A price was put on the heads of President John Taylor and his First Counselor, George Q. Cannon. In a slap at the aging Taylor, a larger reward was offered for the younger Cannon.

justification that he was a lascivious scoundrel), he quickly scurried to Washington and stirred passions to a boil by declaring the Mormons were in open revolt.

President Buchanan sent the U.S. Army to quell the rebellion (see box, below), but the venture failed to resolve the Mormon question. After the Civil War, the focus of the nation once again turned towards the Mormons and polygamy. Federal marshalls with broad powers from Congress pursued polygamists, throwing them in prison by the hundreds. At one point the property of the church was seized and the leadership driven underground. A price was put on the head of Young's successor, John Taylor, who would die in hiding.

Ordinary Mormons grew weary of the struggle. Less than 10% ever practiced plural marriage, and enthusiasm for it began to fade among the rank and file. Statehood was repeatedly denied because of polygamy; business and commerce suffered. In 1890, a new president of the church, Wilford Woodruff, issued "The Manifesto." It ended polygamy among mainstream Mormons.

Utah Historical Society

1,035 polygamists were pursued and jailed by federal marshalls in the 1880s.

Renegade groups, however, still cling to polygamy, occasionally making the evening news. The church is quick to condemn such groups, and Mormons have enthusiastically embraced the traditional definition of marriage and family (see p. 26). In a strange historical twist, no people is more unsympathetic to polygamy than modern Mormons.

For more information on polygamy currently in the news, go to **www.sltrib.com**.

THE UTAH WAR

In 1857, President James Buchanan sent 2500 troops to remove Brigham Young as governor. Mormon raiders burned their supply wagons and drove off livestock, but avoided killing. The harried troops, under the command of Colonel Albert S. Johnston, were forced to winter in Wyoming. In the spring, 30,000 Mormons abandoned their homes in Northern Utah and threatened to burn Salt Lake City to the ground if it was occupied. Negotiations spared both lives and property: the Mormons agreed to a new governor and Johnston's army set up camp far from Mormon towns. The Eastern press dubbed the enterprise "Buchanan's Blunder."

With the outbreak of the Civil War, the Army was recalled. Col. Johnston resigned to accept a commission in the Confederate Army. Once commanded to put down Mormon "rebels" in Utah, Johnston was killed wearing rebel gray at the Battle of Shiloh.

Albert Sydney Johnston was sent to quell the Mormon "rebellion."

SCRIPTURE

What Are the Mormon Scriptures?

The Mormon canon—books revered as divinely inspired—include the Bible, the Doctrine and Covenants, the Pearl of Great Price (see opposite page), and the Book of Mormon. These works define and shape Mormonism. The most important is the Book of Mormon. Since 1830, 120 million copies have been published in 104 languages.

The story of the Book of Mormon is familiar to every Mormon child: in 1823, the Angel Moroni, a prophet who lived in America 1600 years ago, appeared to Joseph Smith. He told Smith of a history written on golden plates that was buried in a nearby hill. Joseph was shown the plates, but forbidden from acquiring them until 1827. Using divine artifacts and inspiration, he translated the plates and published the resulting work in 1830 as the Book of Mormon.

So what does this ancient history say? In 600 B.C. a group of Hebrews fled Jerusalem before its destruction by the Babylonians. They built a ship and—miraculously guided by the Spirit—landed in America, where they soon split into two rival groups—the Nephites and the Lamanites.

Generally, the Lamanites were fallen and depraved, descending into a kind of barbarism, while the Nephites were enlightened and God-fearing. However, the ebb and flow of the story includes several reversals, with the Lamanites sometimes accepting the Word of God while the Nephites became idolatrous. The message of the book, however, remains constant—a people who adheres to the Word of God prospers, while those who reject His prophets and His message fall into ignorance and darkness.

PFB

A facsimile of the gold plates. Mormons believe they contained a history, which Smith translated into the Book of Mormon.

When Jesus was crucified in Jerusalem, the inhabitants of the Americas suffered cataclysmic disasters. Floods, earthquakes and fires from Heaven destroyed entire cities, followed by three days and nights of total blackness. The darkness was dispelled when Jesus descended from Heaven on the third day. He healed and taught the survivors, who were allowed to approach and touch Him, so they would know He was real. After establishing His church, He departed. Two hundred years of peace followed.

In time, dissensions arose and people once again split into Nephites and Lamanites. A last, great battle in 384 A.D. annihilated the Nephites forever. The victorious Lamanites split into warring groups, becoming the Indian tribes Columbus encountered a thousand years later.

The last survivor of the Nephite nation, Moroni, was entrusted with a history

Utah Historical Society

Smith, receiving the plates from the Angel Moroni.

THE DOCTRINE AND COVENANTS

The Doctrine and Covenants is the constitution of the Mormon Church, or "a collection of divine revelations and inspired declarations given for the establishment and regulation of the kingdom of God on the earth in the last days," according to Joseph Smith. The book is divided into sections, the bulk of which are revelations given by God, through Smith, to His church. It also includes more recent revelations, namely "The Manifesto," which ended polygamy, and the "Revelation on Priesthood," which gave blacks the priesthood in 1978 (see p. 25).

engraved on gold plates by his father, Mormon. Moroni buried the plates in a stone box in a hill, where they remained until removed 1400 years later by Smith. The gold plates were returned to Moroni upon completion of the translation. Two-thirds of the plates were sealed by gold bands and Smith was forbidden from opening that portion. Said to contain specific prophecies concerning the last days, the "sealed portion" is supposed to be revealed sometime in the future.

It is Jesus's lost teachings from ancient America that give the Book of Mormon its hallowed place in Mormon belief. In fact, the book bears the subtitle, "Another Testament of Jesus Christ." Jesus delivers a blueprint on how to achieve a righteous life and a righteous community. The mission of the Mormon Church is to once again foster a righteous people and a time of peace like that in the Book of Mormon.

Critics point to anachronisms in the Book of Mormon as evidence of its questionable authenticity. Elephants, steel and horses are mentioned, but their existence in the Americas is not yet proven by archaeological evidence. Recent DNA studies also fail to validate a Hebrew presence in the New World.

Mormons respond that no one could have written such a complex and powerful narrative—much less someone raised on the frontier with only a sketchy formal education—unless they were inspired. They also cite archaeological evidence. Cement, mentioned in the Book of Mormon, was found in ancient American sites after the book was published. In any case, belief in the book is held to be a matter of faith that can only be gained through sincere meditation and prayer.

The complete texts of the Mormon scriptures can be accessed at www.scriptures.lds.org

PFB

In 1835, Smith came into possession of four Egyptian mummies and papyri. He attested the writings were of the biblical patriarchs Abraham and Joseph of Egypt. Smith's inspired translation of the hieroglyphics comprises the heart of the Pearl of Great Price, which is one of the church's standard works. Some non-Mormon scholars offer a different explanation, that the writings are funerary texts, common to Egyptian ceremonial mummifications and burials

THE BIBLE

Mormons share the same reverence for the Bible as the rest of Christianity. The King James Bible is the officially accepted English language version. Newer translations are viewed with skepticism and their use is discouraged. Generally, Mormons take a literal approach to the Bible—there really was an Adam and Eve and a Garden of Eden. The miracles described in the Old and New Testaments are taken at face value.

However, Mormonism can be pragmatic in its reading of Bible stories. Some are seen as allegorical. For instance, the creation of the world in six days is taken to mean six periods of time. Many Mormons are comfortable with an earth that is billions of years old. Likewise, the question of biological evolution is left open.

PFB

DOCTRINE
What Do Mormons Believe?

The centerpiece of Mormon belief is the "Plan of Salvation," a bird's eye view of where people came from, why they are here, and what happens to the soul after death.

Before the creation of the earth, men and women first existed as "intelligences," and later as spirit children of God. The most glorious of God's children was Jesus Christ, who offered a plan that would permit the rest to grow into spiritual maturity. This meant being born into the physical world to acquire bodies of flesh and blood, but also being stripped of memories of having ever lived in God's presence.

This world is a proving ground where all are free to choose for themselves: good or evil, righteousness or sin. Mormons put a high value on personal responsibility and good works. But faith in Christ is also essential. Daily decisions are often viewed as choices with eternal consequences. The Devil (Satan is a very real entity in Mormon cosmology) and the Holy Ghost are involved in an ongoing struggle to influence the heart of every man and woman.

Prayer offers protection and is essential to help navigate complicated choices and avoid temptation—God hears and answers all sincere prayers. The whisperings of the Spirit, sometimes called "a still, small voice," encourages righteous actions and harmonious living. But giving in to one's natural inclinations leads to spiritual decay, with all its attendant ills: cruelty, selfishness and addiction.

Jesus's earthly sojourn was essentially a rescue mission. His sacrifice saved men and women from spiritual and physical death. Even the most righteous fall short of perfection, and even the best of bodies grow old, frail, and die. Jesus's atonement covers all mankind's sins, and His resurrection—with a perfect, glorified body—makes possible the resurrection of one's own.

PFB

The "Christus" statue, a replica of the original by Danish artist Bertrel Thorvaldsen, is in the visitors' center on Temple Square in Salt Lake City.

The notion that God has a tangible body strikes many as peculiar. Mormons say their belief that God has an undying, incorruptible body lends dignity to the material universe. In a Mormon universe, even the earth itself will be redeemed and resurrected. In fact, there will be a heaven on the earth because Earth *will* be Heaven.

A person needs a body for "eternal progression," a uniquely Mormon belief that God, like any good parent, is nurturing His children to be more godly. Having a body is an important step in the process of becoming more like Him. In the future course of eternity, advanced individuals may have spirit children of their own. The idea is captured in this popular Mormon couplet: "As man is, God once was. As God is, man may become."

At death, men and women find themselves in the "spirit world," where the Gospel continues to be preached. They are still themselves, with the same prejudices, habits and beliefs held in this life.

When Christ returns to the earth in glory (see box, opposite), there will be a general resurrection and the

HEAVEN

Beliefs about the afterlife usually involve a heaven for the righteous and a hell for the wicked. The Mormon story of what happens beyond the grave is more nuanced. It allows for more than a one-size-fits-all paradise.

Called the "Three Degrees of Glory," Mormon Heaven is essentially God grading on a curve. Virtually everyone is saved in one of three kingdoms, whose relative glories are represented by the sun (Celestial Kingdom), the moon (Terrestrial Kingdom) and the stars (Telestial Kingdom). Within each of the kingdoms, there are said to be even further gradations. It's an optimistic take on the next life; even the Telestial Kingdom is described as a place of light and glory.

PFB

"kingdom of God on the earth" will be established for a thousand years. The veil that separates Heaven and Earth will be stretched thin to the point that resurrected beings will pass between this world and the next. At the end of the thousand years, Satan will lash out one last time in an attempt to destroy Christ's kingdom. He will be defeated and banished forever to "outer darkness," along with his most depraved minions.

Some Christian groups view Mormonism as a dangerous heresy, arguing that Mormons are not Christian. The Book of Mormon and a living Mormon prophet in Salt Lake City, whose words carry the weight of scripture, are seen as undermining the authority of the Bible. The doctrine of eternal progression, they assert, is nothing more than pagan polytheism.

But Mormons say they affirm traditional Christian doctrines. The "good news" of the Gospel—that faith in Christ is essential to salvation—is basic Mormon doctrine. Christ's life and teachings from the New Testament are central to their beliefs. To underscore the point, in 1981 a subtitle was added to the Book of Mormon: "Another Testament of Jesus Christ."

Mormons choose to emphasize the life-affirming aspects of the resurrection rather than the crucifixion, which is why the cross is conspicuously absent from Mormon buildings.

To learn more about Mormon doctrine, visit **www.mormon.org**.

Some Christian groups claim that Mormon doctrine is heretical and Mormons are not Christians. Here, evangelical street preachers proselyte attendees at Mormon General Conference in Salt Lake City.

Dan Thomas

THE SECOND COMING

Unlike Christ's first incarnation, when He arrived as a babe in a Judean stable, His second coming will be in power and glory. He will establish His kingdom among the few left untouched by the overwhelming wickedness that will have engulfed the earth. The wicked will be destroyed and the righteous will join Jesus for a thousand years of peace.

The name "Latter-day Saints" indicates the Mormon belief that these are indeed the last days of this world. Joseph Smith and subsequent leaders have preached that Jesus's coming is imminent. Members are encouraged to store food and supplies to weather the dark days that will precede Christ's return. But they pragmatically engage in planning for an ordinary future, having been advised, "pray as though Jesus were coming tomorrow, but go ahead and plant your apple trees."

PFB

RITES & RULES

What Are Mormon Laws?

All religions have rites and rules of conduct, or commandments, that the faithful are expected to follow. But few can match Mormonism for the level of dedication required to stay right with God.

Faith, repentance, baptism and the Gift of the Holy Ghost are the first principles of the Gospel and bind one to the body of the church. Baptism (see box, below) into the Mormon Church means leaving an old life behind and entering into a new one. The new life includes rules and observances that, if faithfully followed in the proper spirit, lead to closer communion with God.

The commandments touch every aspect of daily living. Starting with the Ten Commandments, Mormons obey a host of others: weekly church attendance, heeding the leaders of the church, loving one's neighbor, following the Word of Wisdom, striving to keeps one's thoughts pure, scripture study, monthly fasts, and daily prayer to deepen one's relationship with God.

Satan tries to seduce men and women with promises of easy fulfillment. Instant gratification is his most potent weapon. Mormons arm themselves against temptation with obedience to God's Word. His commandments are meant to stiffen one's spiritual spine.

Putting one's money where one's faith is is expected of all faithful Mormons. Tithing is a law that asks 10% of a person's income. Compliance is voluntary, but the fact that Utah ranks highest in charitable contributions indicates Mormons take this law seriously. The first Sunday of the month is "Fast Sunday." Mormons fast for two meals and donate the money saved to a fast offering for fellow Mormons in need. Fast Sunday is also an opportunity to stand before the congregation and affirm belief in the divine mission of the church.

Mormons believe the Ten Commandments are the foundation of moral law.

BAPTISM

Baptism is an ordinance necessary for salvation. Mormons practice "total immersion," the act of being briefly, but totally, submerged in water. As with the rest of Christianity, baptism represents a new birth and the washing away of old sins. However, the baptisms of other churches are not recognized by the Mormon Church. Those wishing to join the church must be baptized according to the Mormon rite.

The young are baptized upon reaching what is called the "age of accountability," eight years old—presumably old enough to choose between right and wrong. Children who die before are considered blameless and do not require baptism to be saved.

LDS Church Archives

FAITH HEALING

Mormons believe in modern medicine, but also put their faith in priesthood blessings. Elders are often called on to anoint the sick and give healing blessings. This involves an anointing with consecrated oil, followed by "the laying on of hands." Such blessings are administered as a supplement to traditional medical treatments. Medical advances are esteemed as gifts of God, and skipping these for a faith-only approach is considered unnecessarily foolish. However, most Mormons are able to cite instances of miraculous priesthood healings when doctors had given up on a cure.

Weekly attendance at Sunday services is a keenly felt obligation. At Sacrament Meeting, the most important meeting of the week, Mormons partake of a sacrament of bread and water, much like communion. Intended to call to mind the sacrifice of Christ, the sacrament is a reminder to live the Gospel.

Mormons are great believers in the virtue of scripture study. Many begin or end their day with an open book, pondering the Word of God. It is one way— prayer being another—to open oneself to inspiration from the Spirit.

Originally delivered as merely good advice, the Word of Wisdom is now one of the defining characteristics of what it is to be a Mormon. The Word of Wisdom was a revelation given to Joseph Smith in 1833. Since the 1930s, it has been interpreted to mean total abstinence from coffee, tea, alcohol and tobacco. Abuse of drugs, whether prescription or otherwise, is also forbidden. Studies show living this law has definite benefits: Mormons live longer and are healthier than their neighbors. For instance, Utah, which is 75% Mormon, has the lowest cancer rate in the nation.

Mormons see the difficulty of living their religion as evidence that theirs is the true church. They respond to the evils of the world with wholesome dedication. As President Joseph Fielding Smith said, "It is one thing to give lip service to the Lord; it is quite another to respect and honor His will by following the example He has set for us."

The rigors of living the laws of Mormonism are not for everyone. Many can't see the sense of God wanting them to give up their morning cup of coffee. Mormons who fall short or lack dedication are called "Jack Mormons."

PFB

Mormons believe the body is a temple. The Word of Wisdom is the Mormon dietary law which prohibits tea and coffee, tobacco, and alcoholic beverages.

SEX AND MORMONS

Mormons are proudly old-fashioned when it comes to sex. While sexual pleasure is meant to be enjoyed, relations outside of marriage are strictly forbidden. A Duke University study found that Mormons are least likely to cohabitate outside of marriage: 8% compared with 20-24% for Protestants, 23% for Catholics, and 45% for non-religious Americans.

Adultery is as deadly a sin as a Mormon can commit, scarcely less serious than murder. The offending party is often excommunicated—he or she is denied the sacrament. Readmittance to the fold is possible after an arduous process that demonstrates sincere repentance.

Single Mormons are expected to remain celibate until marriage. Other sexual activities, such as masturbation and intimate touching, are also frowned upon. Homosexual sex is forbidden under any circumstance. Those who feel same-sex attraction are counseled to lead a celibate life.

Contraception is left for couples to decide, though morning-after methods are forbidden. Parenthood is a sacred obligation. Bringing spirits into this world is every healthy Mormon couple's responsibility.

Unwed girls who become pregnant often choose to place their baby with a Mormon couple through the church's social services. Abortion is countenanced, but only in the rare instances of rape, incest, and when the life and health of the mother is at risk.

19

MISSIONARIES

What's With the White Shirts and Ties?

Wherever you go, there they are: earnest pairs of young men in white shirts and ties. They can be seen in every corner of the globe, walking or bicycling their way to spread the good news that the blessings of a happy and fulfilling life are available to everyone through His true church. 60,000 missionaries are currently preaching in 141 countries around the world. Ironically, these well-scrubbed adolescents—only recently acquainted with a razor—are called "elders."

As in the military, elders serve where they are sent. But unlike the military, they are told they are God's ambassadors on earth. They make a commitment at 19 years of age to set aside the things that normally engage the attention of young men—girls, college, career, cars, sports—and dedicate themselves for two years to spreading the Gospel.

Missionaries are assigned to work in pairs, or "companionships," that must stay together 24 hours a day, until reassigned. Companions live, eat, pray, proselytize and sleep within mere feet of each other. While fast friendships are often formed, missionaries wryly observe that such unremitting closeness is a great opportunity for developing Christian charity.

A missionary's life is as rigorously disciplined as any monk's. Every fifteen minute block of time during the day is scheduled. At 6:30 a.m. the missionary is up to shave, shower, dress, study scriptures, eat breakfast and pray before hitting the streets at 8:00. There is time for lunch and dinner, otherwise the rest of the day is dedicated to proselytizing until bed time at precisely 10:30 p.m. It is an 80 hour work week.

One day a week is reserved to do laundry, write letters home, and perhaps play a game of "hoop" with other missionaries. Time is also made for community service not involving proselytizing.

Rules governing conduct are listed in a small, white book that missionaries call "The White Bible." It forbids music, movies, swimming and unauthorized reading material. Even casual contact with members of the opposite sex is discouraged, and dating is grounds for being sent home in disgrace. Dress is dictated as well: dark business suits, though in hot climates, a white shirt and slacks may be acceptable. Enforcing all these rules is the mission president, a married adult who has the unenviable task of looking after the welfare of a hundred or so very young people.

PFB

Mormon missionaries are found the world over. Called "elders," they serve for two years.

Early Mormonism realized spectacular mass conversions through its missionary program, which is nearly as old as the church itself. Wilford Woodruff converted thousands in England in the 1840s, including a constable who had been sent to arrest him for disturbing the peace.

CONVERSION

People not born into the faith come to Mormonism's doorstep in various ways: a family member, a friendly co-worker, or a knock on the door from two fresh-faced young men. In any case, baptism into the Mormon Church lies through study, prayer and prepared lessons from the missionaries. The missionary discussions are a quick, concise course designed to acquaint one with the beliefs and obligations of Mormonism. Having completed the discussions, one is prepared for baptism (see p. 18) and full membership in the church.

10,500,000 members

Single female Mormons may serve as "lady missionaries" for eighteen months.

PFB

Missionaries, or their families, pay for the privilege of serving. The church may help disadvantaged elders, but those with resources contribute to a missionary fund. Frugality is stressed, as the elder's living allowance belongs to the Lord.

The mission experience is not limited to young men. 17% of missionaries are women. "Lady missionaries" may serve if they are 21. Lacking priesthood, they nonetheless bring maturity and dedication to their endeavors. Prospective converts that do not respond to male missionaries may find "the Sisters" less threatening. Older, retired couples are also becoming important to the missionary program. Called to serve together, these husbands and wives staff church visitors' centers and serve in other areas where their experience is an asset.

The missionary program has been a spectacular success. It took the Mormon Church 120 years to reach 1 million members. The second million took only 16 years. Today, there are 12 million members listed on the rolls. The church owes much of its phenomenal growth to young missionaries. What's more, at the end of two years, these superbly trained and motivated young Mormons are ready to step into leadership positions in their home wards.

58,000 missionaries

Many young men and women devote themselves to spreading the Gospel full-time, but the saying, "Every member a missionary," indicates it is a duty of all Mormons.

LDS Church Archives

Five Million	
Fifty Thousand	
Four Million	
Forty Thousand	
Three Million	**CHURCH POPULATION**
Thirty Thousand	**and**
Two Million	**MISSIONARIES**
Twenty Thousand	
	CHURCH MEMBERSHIP
One Million	
Ten Thousand	

CHURCH POPULATION and MISSIONARIES

CHURCH MEMBERSHIP

1964
second million
members

1947
first million
members

MISSIONARIES

283,765
members

WW II

1960
9,000
missionaries

1830   1900   2000

T E M P L E S

What Are Mormon Temples For?

Much of what goes on in Mormon temples is regarded by the faithful as too holy to be discussed outside the precincts of the temple. Mormons are sensitive to charges that they are keeping secrets, saying that what goes on in the temple is sacred, not secret. In either case, outsiders are left to wonder.

At the turn of the 20th century, Congress was sufficiently suspicious to insist on a full disclosure of the temple ceremonies. What they found disappointed fevered anti-Mormon fantasies—no orgies, pagan rituals or blood sacrifices. The Mormons were permitted to freely continue their temple practices in peace.

Traditionally, the building of temples have been undertakings that call on the resources and talents of the entire community. It is a physical expression of a people's devotion. The Salt Lake Temple, for example, took 40 years to complete, at a time when the Mormons were often scraping by on subsistence farming. Modern temples today are built more rapidly, but are still revered in the areas they serve. Some, like the temple in Washington D.C., are well-known local landmarks.

A temple is the most sacred building in Mormonism. It represents a place where Heaven touches Earth. It is where worthy Mormons more directly learn godliness.

Admittance to the temple is restricted to worthy members of the church. Worthiness is determined through interviews with local church leaders who ask a series of prepared questions. Fidelity, honesty and moderation are at the heart of the interview.

In the temple, Mormons receive their "endowments." Mormons believe the endowment harks back to the sacred ordinances of ancient biblical patriarchs. It is bestowed in a ritual reserved for adult Mormons who promise to fully commit themselves to serve God. Disclosing the particulars of this sacred ceremony is especially insulting to faithful Mormons.

PFB

Mormonism's most recognized symbol, the Salt Lake Temple, was completed in 1893. The walls at the base are 12 feet thick.

As of 2004, there were 119 Mormon temples throughout the world. Some are architectural landmarks that boldly proclaim the presence of the new American-born faith. Other, more modest edifices allow small Mormon communities a place where the blessings of the temple can be enjoyed. View a complete list of temples at **www.lds.org/temples**.

Mormon temple in Bern, Switzerland

Couples who have received their endowments and wish to marry for "time and all eternity" may be "sealed" in Mormon temples. Such a union between a man and woman continues into the next life, and is an essential step for exaltation.

Mormons who have their endowments wear special underclothes called garments, which resemble ordinary undershirts and briefs. They remind one of covenants made in the temple. Rumors that Mormons *never* remove the garments—even to bathe—are not true. Mormons are ever-practical, especially concerning hygiene.

The temple ceremony was one of the final ordinances that Joseph Smith bequeathed to the church. His successors faithfully carried the tradition of temple-building and temple work with them across the plains. In Utah, the pioneers were quick to build a temporary Endowment House to perform their sacred ceremonies. It was torn down when the Salt Lake Temple was dedicated in 1893.

The figure atop many temples is the Book of Mormon prophet, Moroni, heralding the restoration of the Gospel. This gold-leafed statue on the Salt Lake Temple is 13 feet tall.

PFB

GENEALOGY

Concern for the souls of one's ancestors is at the heart of Mormons' interest in genealogy. A record that an ancestor existed is necessary for that ancestor's temple work to be done (see box, below). As a result, Mormons are famous for combing through court records and parish registries to reconstruct family trees. Diligent research is sometimes rewarded with the discovery of someone famous hiding on a branch—a U.S. president, European royalty, or maybe a notorious outlaw.

PFB

Millions of microfilm records are stored in a specially constructed vault drilled into a granite mountain near Salt Lake City. These serve as the basis for the largest genealogical data base in the world, with over 700 million listings and 2 billion names! Much of it can be accessed by the public at **www.FamilySearch.org**.

WORK FOR THE DEAD

Temple blessings are not restricted to the living. A doctrine unique to Mormonism asserts that those who have died without hearing the Gospel will have the opportunity not only to hear it in the afterlife, but to be baptized by proxy. In special temple fonts, living volunteers are baptized on behalf of the deceased. Temple endowments are also performed for the dead, the ceremony once again being carried out by a living volunteer who stands in for someone waiting in the afterlife.

Proxy baptisms for the dead take place in special fonts supported on twelve oxen statues representing the twelve tribes of Israel.

PFB

A LIVING PROPHET

Does God Still Speak Today?

Authority is an important concept in Mormonism. It is the difference between pretending to speak for God and being legitimately ordained to act on His behalf.

Just as prophets spoke for God in biblical times, Mormons look to a living prophet to speak for Him today. The acknowledged leader of Mormons is the president of the church, who is believed to be chosen by God to act as His spokesman. He also bears the title of Prophet, Seer and Revelator, though known universally throughout the church as "The Prophet."

The Prophet is thought to live closer to God than anyone on earth. Former presidents have often drawn the distinction between speaking as a man and speaking as a prophet. When speaking as a prophet, the president is incapable of leading the church into error. He has two counselors who act as vice presidents. Together, these three make up the First Presidency.

The Salt Lake Tribune

As the church entered the 21st century, Gordon B. Hinckley was the Prophet, Seer and Revelator for over 10 million Mormons. Here, he is interviewed by talk show host Larry King.

The Quorum of the Twelve Apostles is a kind of board of directors that assists the First Presidency. "The Twelve" is responsible for the missionary program and various aspects of church governance. The Twelve are also called "apostles," like those of Jesus's time.

Apostle Reed Smoot

Some members of the Twelve have been distinguished public figures. Reed Smoot, an apostle in the early 20th century, was also a powerful U.S. senator. Ezra Taft Benson, who would become the president of the church in the 1980s, was Secretary of Agriculture in the Dwight D. Eisenhower administration.

The president of the church serves for life, as do the apostles. When the president dies, the First Presidency is dissolved and the Twelve assumes temporary leadership. Even though members of this body go through the motions of electing a new president, custom dictates that the longest serving member of the Twelve is chosen and assumes the mantle of Prophet, Seer and Revelator. As of 2004, there have been 15 presidents of the church.

The Mormon Church has been remarkably free of the dissent and divisions that afflict other religions of similar size. It's hard even to detect the fault lines upon which a major schism might take place. Differences of opinion among the Mormon

MORMON PRIESTHOOD

Mormons trace their priesthood authority to Joseph Smith, who received it from angelic beings. The Aaronic (lesser) Priesthood came at the hands of John the Baptist, and the Melchizedek (higher) Priesthood from Peter, James and John. Priesthood is the authority to act in God's name, under the supervision of the church.

Worthy males are ordained into the Aaronic priesthood at 12 years of age. If they faithfully fulfill their lesser priesthood responsibilities—which include preparing and blessing the sacrament, collecting contributions for the poor called fast offerings, and baptizing—they are ordained into the Melchizedek Priesthood at 18.

One who holds this higher priesthood is often addressed as "Elder." It is a title, much like "Mr.," used for everyone from young missionaries to older apostles.

Ordination to the priesthood is through a ceremony called "the laying on of hands." Adolescents as young as 12 are ordained into the priesthood as "deacons."

PFB

hierarchy are never publicly aired. Decisions of the First Presidency and the Twelve are presented to the membership as unanimous. Consensus is highly valued—Mormons believe dissension is inspired by the Devil and opposition to church leaders is a sign of apostasy. Loyal Mormons, while free to pray for enlightenment, steadfastly support the leaders that God has appointed to guide them.

To govern a rapidly growing church, other churchwide assemblies have become important auxiliaries to the First Presidency and the Twelve. The most important of these are the Quorums of the Seventy, which have as many as 70 members. Currently, there are five such quorums.

Members of any of the ruling councils are known as "general authorities" and occupy esteemed positions of leadership. The church also depends on a professional bureaucracy (see p. 35) and an unpaid clergy (see box, above) to administer to its worldwide congregations and programs.

Background right: The Conference Center, where the membership receives counsel from church leadership at General Conference. Foreground: The Quorum of the Twelve Apostles.

LDS Church Archives

WHO CAN HOLD THE PRIESTHOOD?

From the time of Joseph Smith, men of African descent were barred from holding the Mormon priesthood. All that changed In 1978, when President Spencer Kimball received a revelation overturning a century and a half of church policy. Since then, men of African descent now may bear the same priesthood and positions as all other worthy Mormon males.

The scope of Mormon women's responsibilities in the church has grown in recent decades, reflecting broader social changes. But the conservative nature of Mormonism makes it doubtful there will ever be a revelation giving women the priesthood.

FAMILY VALUES

What Are Mormon Family Values?

Mormonism is a family-centered faith. President David O. McKay said, "no other success can compensate for failure in the home." The long view of eternity and the importance of family is captured in what has become a Mormon creed: "Families are Forever" (see box, opposite).

Mormons aspire to a traditional ideal of family life: a working father who, by virtue of his priesthood, is the head of the household, and a wife who strives to create a loving environment in the home. Church leaders encourage women to be stay-at-home moms: motherhood is more important than a fast-track career.

In theory, it is a clearly defined partnership catering to each other's strengths. In practice, Mormon households make pragmatic choices to fit modern realities. Statistics show Mormon women enter the workforce at the same rate as other Americans. Stay-at-home dads, working moms and adult children living at home are all national trends echoed in Mormon households.

Children are taught respect and responsibility. From an early age, lessons on the difference between right and wrong, good and evil, are learned in the home and reinforced in church. Obedience to God's commandments and respect for authority are the bedrock of juvenile instruction.

Mormon families are famously large, about twice the U.S. average. The baby boom that swept America in the '50s never really went out of style with Mormons. National trends to marry and have

Family Home Evening promotes family togetherness.

PFB

PROCLAMATION ON THE FAMILY

In 1995, the Mormon Church issued "The Family: A Proclamation to the World," a clarion call for Mormons to become politically involved in their communities to protect the institution of marriage. Failure on this front could unleash global calamities foretold by God's prophets.

The proclamation reaffirms marriage as an institution ordained by God, in which a man and woman commit to a life together. Only within the bonds of marriage may couples fulfill the biblical obligation to "multiply and replenish the earth." It is a shelter for nurturing children.

Marriage does not, however, allow for non-traditional unions. The proclamation makes clear that same-sex marriages are contrary to God's plan, and encourages members to work for laws that "strengthen the family as the fundamental unit of society." Abuses within marriage, such as adultery, and spousal and child abuse, are also condemned.

ETERNAL FAMILIES

"Families are forever" is a saying minted and marketed by Mormons. It is an attractive selling point to prospective converts who find comfort and connection in family. But it is more than a clever slogan. Mormons believe the ties that bind a person to loved ones existed before this life, and will continue after death. The family relationships in this life were perhaps agreed upon in the premortal existence. And family ties are stronger than death. Unless one is lost to sin or transgression, Mormons expect to be reunited in some form of family unit forever.

children later in life barely register among Mormons. Census figures show that Utah is host to 9 of the 10 youngest counties in the nation. This phenomenon inspires self-depre-cating jokes that Mormons tell on themselves. For instance, family-friendly minivans are referred to as Mormon Assault Vehicles.

The penchant for large families can be traced to the pioneer past, when numerous children were an asset on a working farm. But it also comes from a belief that spirits waiting to come to this world will be sent elsewhere if not born into Mormon house-holds. Children born to couples sealed in the temple are said to be born "under the covenant."

Mormons who marry in the temple have dramatically lower rates of divorce. Whereas half of all U.S. marriages fail, only about 6% of temple-solemnized marriages do. Curiously, Mormons who have civil marriages have the same divorce rates as other Americans. And divorce rates of Mormons who marry outside their faith are among the highest of any religious group.

PFB

Children are taught the importance of prayer and morals at an early age.

Monday night in Mormon households is "Family Home Evening." As the name suggests, it is a time set aside in the hectic work week to spend with one's family. Family Home Evening can involve games, gospel lessons, or a pow-wow to work out problems. It has been rec-ognized as a huge success in promoting family unity. National family groups have even created their own programs based on the Mormon model.

Despite the wholesome image, Mormon families are not immune to life's trials. Depression, abuse, neglect, infidelity and drug abuse can strike Mormon households. The church takes a proactive approach to these modern plagues. It operates a professional social services department that networks with local church leaders to help members in need of coun-seling or support. Mormons are committed to building self-sufficient communities that take care of their own.

DATING AND MARRIAGE

In a culture so family oriented, single Mormons are eager to find that special someone with whom to spend eternity. To help nature take its course, the church sponsors singles wards, congregations where unmarried Mormons meet, socialize, and hopefully marry someone with similar goals and values. 21st century technology has also been harnessed to help find that eternal soulmate. Popular internet sites for Mormons-seeking-same include **LDSsingles.com, LDSmingle.com,** and **SingleSaints.com**.

Higher advancement in the church is blocked to diehard bache-lors. From bishops to the president, church officials are husbands and usually fathers. Single Mormon males are often reminded by well-meaning aunts and uncles of Brigham Young's warn-ing that unmarried men over 21 are a menace to society. Pressure to marry can be intense, which isn't made easi-er by the realization that such a union is eternal.

PFB

COMMUNITY

What Is The Secret of Mormon Unity?

Mormons proudly assert that "the church is the same, no matter where you go." Whether in Poland or Pasadena, members address each other as "Brother" and "Sister," are familiar with the same church lingo, look to the same prophet in Salt Lake City for guidance, share the same manner of addressing God in prayer, and go to the same meetings on Sunday. Uniformity of church architecture, behavior, dress and belief all add to the sense of belonging.

The heart of a Mormon community is the ward. Wards are the rough equivalent of parishes and each numbers between 300 and 500 souls. As of 2000, there were 26,000 wards found in every corner of the globe. In remote areas, Mormons may be forced to travel hours to attend Sunday services, whereas in densely Mormon Utah, the ward may encompass a single neighborhood, with the wardhouse just around the corner.

PFB

The wardhouse is the spiritual and cultural center of Mormon community.

From the beginning, Mormons fostered unusually tight-knit communities. The 1870s saw the establishment of 200 United Orders, an experiment in communalism in which members of entire towns held all things in common. Most were organized to pool property and capital so members could share in the profits. Some of these Mormon utopias experienced short-lived success, usually lasting only as long as it took to suspect one's neighbor of getting an unfair share. By the 1880s, almost all of the United Orders had failed. But the experience left its mark and is still held up as an ideal to be lived by Mormons in some indefinite future.

Today, the life of the community revolves around the wardhouse. Besides being a house of worship with a chapel, each ward building contains a cultural hall that serves variously as a basketball court, reception center, dining hall and overflow for the chapel.

Sunday services include a variety of meetings for men, women and children. While men and young-adult males go to Priesthood Meeting, women attend Relief Society (see box, opposite). Sunday School has classes for children and adults, all focusing on scripture and moral living. The most important gathering of the day is Sacrament Meeting. Here, the congregation partakes of a sacrament of bread and water and hears talks, or sermonettes, delivered by fellow ward members. Callings to serve in various capacities in the ward can require planning sessions. Often, four hours of meetings can be packed into a single Sunday.

The beehive was adopted by Mormons in Utah to symbolize community and industry. Like the bee, individuals work together for the good of the whole. It is an icon found on the state seal of Utah and the state flag, and is a popular motif on buildings, bedspreads and even manhole covers. Incidentally, Utah-produced honey is said to be uncommonly delicious.

28

PFB

CHURCH WELFARE PROGRAM

The Great Depression of the 1930s hit Utah hard. Unemployment in some rural counties approached 80%. Reluctant to take handouts, the proudly self-reliant Mormons hit on a practical solution. In 1936, the Church Security (later "Welfare") Program was officially launched. Church-owned dairies, farms, orchards and canneries provided both work and welfare for tens of thousands of members in need. The system was studied with great interest by the Franklin D. Roosevelt administration before launching its own government assistance program.

The church also operates secondhand stores similar to Salvation Army shops. Deseret Industries, known as DI, recycles clothing and goods, while at the same time providing dignified employment for the disabled and jobless.

Church doesn't end on Sunday. Every morning before school, teenage Mormons attend early morning religious instruction called Seminary. Once a month, priesthood holders pair up to home teach. Home teaching is a monthly check-in on ward members to determine their needs. Special programs such as Mutual (a midweek activity for young adults), Boy Scouts and leadership meetings also spill over into the week, making repeat visits to the wardhouse common. Mormons, it seems, would rather be dead than not busy.

Mormon congregations sponsor thousands of Boy Scout troops.

The leader of the ward is the bishop, who is appointed from among the ward members. It is full-time work on top of holding down a day job. A good bishop is part counselor, referee, social worker and holy man; all performed with dedication and without pay. He has invaluable help from his two counselors (the three make up the Bishopric), the Elder's Quorum President and the Relief Society President (see box, below). Bishops serve until they are "released," usually after three to five years. Countless other ward duties—teachers, nursery supervisors, records clerks, youth leaders, priesthood positions—are also staffed by ward members.

The Church Correlation Program, run out of headquarters in Salt Lake City (see p. 35), provides teaching guides that guarantee Mormons around the world are literally on the same page on any given Sunday. Lessons on the Book of Mormon, the Bible, sacred history, and gospel living are developed and coordinated for global congregations from Salt Lake City.

The ward is a ready-made social network that provides everything from baby-sitting to help finding a job. Moving to a new city half-way across the country is no problem. A call to the local ward brings out volunteers who haul the couch into your new home on the way to becoming your new best friends.

PFB

It's been observed that Mormon communities tend to be exclusive. Though not forbidden, Mormons are discouraged from dating and marrying outside their faith. But members go out of their way to make visitors to the ward feel welcome. In an outreach effort to non-Mormons, missionaries volunteer one day a week for community service. The church encourages members to get involved and make positive contributions to the life of their neighborhoods and home towns.

The Mormon Church sponsors a web site that offers advice on everything from healthy living to employment opportunities. Visit **www.ProvidentLiving.org**.

WOMEN AND THE CHURCH

In 1842, Joseph Smith's wife, Emma Hale, headed a new women's organization to help the poor and promote moral rectitude. The Female Relief Society, now called simply the Relief Society, is one of the oldest women's organizations in the world.

Each ward has a Relief Society with a president—the most prestigious and taxing position a woman can hold in the ward. The Relief Society today focuses on instruction in making the home a haven from the evil influences of the world, while also taking the lead in caring for members in moments of crisis. Mormon women take seriously their religious obligation to care for the sick and destitute.

The Salt Lake Tribune

FAMOUS MORMONS

Do You Know Any Mormons?

The contributions Mormons have made to art, science, sports, literature, business and culture far exceed their numbers.

Did you know the Maytag Man was a Mormon? **Gordon Jump**, who played Ol' Lonely from 1987-2003, was also well known as Arthur Carlson, the befuddled station manager at "WKRP in Cincinnati." Other Mormon actors include **Rick Schroder** ("Silver Spoons," "NYPD Blue"), **Matthew Modine** ("Full Metal Jacket"), **Keene Curtis** (*The Rothschilds*, *Annie*), **Aaron Eckhart** ("Posession"), and director **Neil LaBute** ("Your Friends and Neighbors").

Do you remember **The Osmonds**? Led by siblings **Donny** and **Marie**, the Ogden, Utah family scored 28 gold records in the '70s, making the Osmond name synonymous with wholesome, family entertainment. Mormons are no strangers to rock and roll either. **Warren Zevon** and **Randy Bachman** (The Guess Who and B.T.O.) both come from Mormon backgrounds. Soul legend **Gladys Knight** became a member in the '90s.

There have been two Mormon Miss Americas: **Colleen Hutchins** (1951) and **Sharlene Wells** (1984). Wells, now Sharlene Hawkes, became a sports broadcaster with ESPN. If you've seen her on TV, you have another Mormon to thank. **Philo T. Farnsworth** first got the idea for "the tube" at age 14. He showed his design to his chemistry teacher, but it took Farnsworth seven years to finally patent his television in 1927.

Steve Young—a descendant of Brigham Young—led the San Francisco 49ers to two Super Bowl Championships and set a string of NFL records. Hall of Famer **Merlin Olsen** was a member of the Los Angeles Rams' "Fearsome Foursome" in the '60s. After terrorizing quarterbacks, he had success in broadcasting and television (remember him in "Little House on the Prairie?"). Other Mormon greats include baseball's **Harmon Killebrew**, **Dale Murphy** and **Wally Joyner**; golfers **Johnny Miller** and **Billy Casper**; boxer **Gene Fullmer**; wrestling superstar **Jimmy "Super Fly" Snuka**, and Boston Celtics sharpshooter **Danny Ainge**.

Recently, Mormon writers have captured the imagination of millions. **Orson Scott Card** secured himself in the science fiction elite with the award-winning *Ender's Game* series. English writer **Anne Perry** has over 8 million books in print, most notably her popular mystery series set in Victorian England.

Laurel Thatcher Ulrich won the Pulitzer Prize for history with her groudbreaking book, *A Midwife's Tale*. Another Pulitzer winner was investigative journalist **Jack Anderson**, who got his start at the University of Utah's student paper. He went on to become a legend at *The Washington Post*, where one of his biggest scoops was breaking the CIA plot to assassinate Fidel Castro.

Steve Young, San Francisco 49ers Superbowl quarterback

The Salt Lake Tribune

Outlaw Butch Cassidy was the son of a Mormon bishop.

The Salt Lake Tribune

Inventor Philo T. Farnsworth is credited with the development of television.

J. GOLDEN KIMBALL

Known as the "swearing apostle," J. Golden Kimball was a general authority in the early 20th century who often indulged in colorful language. The first part of his life was spent as a cowboy, where he learned to address cattle "in the only language they understand." When he became a general authority, he found it hard not to slip back into his cowboy ways. He is still popular with the faithful, who love sharing tales of his radioactive wit. For example, he was once sent to persuade the youths of Provo to give up their addiction to profanity. He told them, "You can quit swearing. Hell, I did!"

Utah Historical Society

J. Willard Marriott got his start in 1927, when he opened Hot Shoppe, a barbeque stand in Washington D.C. A few thousand franchises later, Marriott International has become the second-largest lodging and food services company in the world. **Jon Huntsman** became one of the world's richest men in one word: plastics. Huntsman International is still family operated, but it's no mom and pop business. It is the world's largest chemical company. Huntsman has used his fortune to help fund cancer research.

Other billionaires the world over rely on the advice of **Steven Covey**, author of *The Seven Habits of Highly Effective People*. The book has sold 12 million copies, been translated into 32 languages, and spent years on *The New York Times* bestseller list.

Johathan Browning converted in Nauvoo, where he made most of the guns the pioneers took West. He set up shop in Ogden, Utah, but his reputation was soon eclipsed by his son: **John Moses Browning** became the world's premier gun designer, developing the automatic rifle and the machine gun.

Mormonism has also had its bad apples. Born to a devout Mormon family in southern Utah, George Leroy Parker was described by ranchers who employed him as the best shot and best cowboy they ever knew. Most people today know him as **Butch Cassidy**, the legendary western outlaw. Rumor has it he escaped the shoot-out in Bolivia, returned to his home state, and lived to a ripe old age under an alias.

Find other Mormon celebrities at **www.FamousMormons.net**.

The Salt Lake Tribune

Above: soul legend Gladys Knight became a Mormon in the 1990s. Below: character actor Gordon Jump was "Ol' Lonely," the Maytag repairman. He also appeared on episodes of "Starsky and Hutch," "Growing Pains," and "Seinfeld."

The Salt Lake Tribune

Donny and Marie Osmond, immortalized on a toy tambourine

PFB

Sharlene Wells won the Miss America title in 1984.

The Salt Lake Tribune

CULTURE & FOLKLORE

Do You Have to Like Jell-O™ to be Mormon?

Mormonism, like all cultures, has its unique stories, myths, foods, songs, rituals and cultural quirks. While not central to the religion, these help Mormons define and distinguish themselves from the rest of the world.

Green Jell-O is celebrated as *the* Mormon foodstuff—no one knows why. Even Mormons who have no taste for gelatin desserts recognize it as part of their cultural heritage. When word surfaced that Iowans ate more Jell-O per capita, Utahns hurried to the dessert aisle of their local grocer and wrested back the jiggly gelatin crown. The most valuable trading pin of the 2002 Salt Lake City Olympics was the green Jell-O pin. It sold for as much as $300.

Other foods, such as "Mormon Muffins" (see box, below), recall the pioneers who were forced to make the most of the little they had. Recipes tend to rely on the basics (flour, potatoes) and what exotic tidbits the land offered (nuts, herbs and berries).

According to strict Mormons, the Word of Wisdom (see p. 19) forbids not just tea and coffee, but *any* caffeinated drinks, including soft drinks. Liberal Mormons, on the other hand, let their hair down with the occasional Diet Coke.™

PFB

Glass grapes and green Jell-O, two icons of Mormon pop culture

PFB

MORMON MUFFIN RECIPE

Mormon cuisine consists of dishes designed to feed, if not multitudes, then a good portion of the neighborhood. And the neighborhood is happy to eat it up. Mormon cookery uses commonplace ingredients to produce uncommon results. Mormon Muffins are a good example.

2 cups boiling water	5 cups flour
5 tsp. baking soda	1 tsp. salt
1 cup shortening	4 cups all-bran cereal
2 cups sugar	2 cups bran flakes
4 eggs	1 cup walnuts (chopped)
1 qt. buttermilk	

DIRECTIONS: Stir soda into boiling water. Set aside.

Whip shortening and sugar together, then beat eggs slowly into mixture, one at a time. Add buttermilk, flour and salt. Mix well. Slowly add soda water. Fold cereals and walnuts into mixture.

Leave muffin mix in refrigerator overnight (optional).

Fill greased muffin tins about 1/2 full. Bake in preheated oven at 350°F for 25 to 30 minutes. Let cool.

Makes about 4 dozen.

PFB

MORMONS AT THE MOVIES

Mormons first appeared in movies in the 1922 silent film "Trapped by the Mormons." It features a missionary with hypnotic powers snaring unsuspecting young women for his Utah harem—thumbs up on turgid melodrama, thumbs down on historical accuracy. Mormons got a makeover in the 1940 "Brigham Young: Frontiersman." Hollywood once again played fast and loose with the facts, but this time Mormons come off saintly instead of demonic. Look for Vincent Price in a supporting role as Joseph Smith.

Offended by the gratuitous sex and swearing in many of today's popular movies, Mormons pioneered the practice of editing out the offending bits. Cleaned-up versions of "Titanic," "Chicago," and "Saving Private Ryan" are now available nationwide for personal viewing, thanks to an enterprising video store in Orem, Utah.

Mormons are now on the other side of the camera, and a sort of Mormon Hollywood is flourishing. "God's Army," "Brigham City," "Pride and Prejudice," "Napoleon Dynamite" and "Saints and Soldiers" are critically acclaimed Mormon-produced films which have received national distribution.

Check out **LDSfilm.com**.

PFB

When sex, drugs, and rock and roll were turning American culture upside-down, Relief Societies were busy turning out glass grapes (they are actually resin). Made to be a table accent, the fad swept the church in the '60s. Dismissed by some as kitschy junk, authentic Mormon glass grapes now fetch substantial sums in fashionable secondhand stores in Beverly Hills.

World events are given an interesting spin when seen through Mormon eyes. Global communism collapsed so Mormon missionaries could proselytize in former Iron Curtain countries. The turmoil in the Middle East is the long-prophesied work-up to Christ's second coming. The apocalyptic future will also include a reverse trek of Mormons back to Missouri, where they will build the chief temple in Jackson County.

When not burdened by the weight of world-ending cataclysm, Mormons can laugh at themselves. The jokes they tell are self-deprecating, funny and illuminating:

Question: How many Mormons does it take to screw in a light bulb?
Answer: Two. One to screw in the light bulb and one to preside.

Question: Why do Mormon women stop having children at 39?
Answer: Because 40 is just too many!

OH MY HECK!

"Oh my heck!" is an expression favored by Mormons and used to show surprise, delight or aggravation. It's what Mormons say instead of #%*&!!! Swearing is a violation of the Second Commandment, which prohibits taking the Lord's name in vain. In the Mormon view, this includes dirty words. Besides "Oh my heck!," Mormons in times of stress may be heard to say flip, fetch, fudge, jeez, dang, darn or shoot, which evidently pass Second Commandment muster.

The popular Mormon acronym CTR (Choose the Right) serves the same purpose as WWJD (What Would Jesus Do?).

PFB

THE THREE NEPHITES

Every religion has its version of guardian angels. Mormon folklore says there are three Nephites who still wander the earth helping people in distress. They appear as friendly strangers to fix a flat tire, leave an envelope with the mortgage payment, protect a Mormon maiden's virtue, or offer a timely warning to avert disaster. They always disappear before anyone can thank them or ask their names.

33

A GLOBAL CHURCH

Where is Mormonism Headed?

In 1998, the Mormon Church reached two important statistical milestones: the population of Mormons worldwide surpassed 10 million, and more than half of those millions resided outside the United States. The first number is remarkable in that 50 years ago there were only a million Mormons, most living in the Mountain West. The second statistic represents a major demographic shift that is forcing Mormonism to think outside its Rocky Mountain cradle. Practices from Utah's Wasatch Front may not translate to places as far away—both culturally and geographically—as Samoa. So suits and ties for priesthood meetings may give way to white shirts and skirts (lava-lavas) in the South Pacific.

It's sometimes forgotten that early in its history, Mormonism had an international flavor. In the mid-19th century, most of the church's membership was foreign born, being converted emigrants from the British isles and Scandinavia. The third president of the church, John Taylor, was English.

Mormons are supremely confidant in the future of their church. And they have reason to be. They live in a time in which baby-boomer Mormons have seen the population of co-religionists explode ten fold. It is now the fourth largest denomination in the United States, and the world's sixth largest Christian group. Optimistic projections put the number of Mormons at 265 million by 2080. Some social scientists say that the church is on a trajectory that will soon push it into the ranks of major world religions.

For the first half of its existence, Mormonism narrowly dodged disaster. Persecution, schism, starvation, polygamy, armed invasion and bankruptcy very nearly did it in. In the last hundred years, it has gone from strength to strength to become a powerful, respected and wealthy institution (see box, below). National politicians court the Mormon vote, Madison Avenue studies Mormonism's appeal, and the church's explosive growth doesn't show any signs of slowing down. The metamorphosis of Mormonism from a quaint backwater religious curiosity to a major force in global society is truly amazing.

PFB

Attendees at the semi-annual General Conference reflect the growing diversity of the church.

HOW WEALTHY IS THE CHURCH?

The extent of the holdings of the Mormon Church is not known since it is a privately held corporation not subject to public disclosure. However, the total value of its assets has been estimated at $35 billion, with an annual income of $7 billion. According to *Time,* if it were listed in the Fortune 500, it would fall in the middle, a little below Union Carbide but still above Nike and The Gap. The church favors investments in real estate and owns vast tracts of land in Hawaii, Florida and of course, Utah. Concerning the wealth of the church, President Hinckley said, "When all is said and done, the only real wealth of the church is the faith of its people."

MORMON TABERNACLE CHOIR

Ronald Reagan called it "America's Choir." The 360 men and women of the Mormon Tabernacle Choir have performed at five presidential inaugurations, recorded five gold and two platinum records, and continue to be the featured attraction on America's longest running radio program, "Music and the Spoken Word." Existing in some form since 1847, the choir draws on a vast reserve of talent—musical education being as important as learning to read in many Mormon homes.

LDS Church Archives

To a Mormon, however, such success is not surprising—it was foreseen. Prophecy assures Mormons that they will go to "every nation, kindred, tongue and people." They believe the Old Testament prophet Isaiah was talking about them when he saw "a stone, cut from the mountain without hands, which shall fill the earth." They have faith that the truth of their message is irresistible.

But it is not the temperament of Mormons to sit around and wait for the inevitable to just happen. They have a strong commitment to works, and finding ways to "improve each shining moment," in the words of a popular Mormon hymn. Bettering oneself through education has always been a cornerstone of Mormon culture. Utah has one of the highest high school graduation rates and one of the most highly educated populations in the nation. According to *Newsweek*, Salt Lake City is the most plugged-in city in the country, with more personal computers per capita than anywhere else. Brigham Young University in Provo, Utah, is engaged in educating a bright, dedicated generation of young leaders to see the church well into the new millennium. 50,000 students are enrolled at BYU and its satellite campuses. Its alumni are found in high levels of business and government, and some are conspicuously engaged in the national debate over values.

The genius of Mormonism is its people. Wherever a Mormon goes, there goes a living testament to the faith. Many who come to Mormonism are converted by the message, but their first impressions invariably come from contact with a Mormon: a coworker with a happy family life, a friendly clerk, or a pair of clean-cut young men at the front door. That the religion lives through its people is appropriate, and in the final analysis, the best judge of Mormonism.

The 1,500,000 sq. ft. Conference Center in Salt Lake City is the largest religious structure in the Americas.

PFB

PFB

CHURCH BUREAUCRACY

The administrative center of The Church of Jesus Christ of Latter-day Saints is in Salt Lake City. The Church Office Building, located next to Temple Square, is a 750,000 sq. ft. building that houses the various agencies necessary to run the temporal side of a booming global religion. The church employs thousands who bring their skills to bear on the complex task of running a global church.

THE 13 ARTICLES OF FAITH

In 1842, Joseph Smith drafted a letter to a Chicago reporter named Wentworth. It contained a declaration of core Mormon beliefs, distilled into 13 articles. The 13 Articles of Faith from the Wentworth letter came to be included in the Mormon canon of scripture, The Pearl of Great Price.

1. We believe in God the Eternal Father, and in His Son, Jesus Christ, and in the Holy Ghost.

2. We believe that men will be punished for their own sins, and not for Adam's transgression.

3. We believe that through the Atonement of Christ, all mankind may be saved, by obedience to the laws and ordinances of the Gospel.

4. We believe that the first principles and ordinances of the Gospel are: first, Faith in the Lord Jesus Christ; second, Repentance; third, Baptism by immersion for the remission of sins; fourth, Laying on of hands for the gift of the Holy Ghost.

5. We believe that a man must be called of God, by prophecy, and by the laying on of hands by those who are in authority, to preach the Gospel and administer in the ordinances thereof.

6. We believe in the same organization that existed in the Primitive Church, namely, apostles, prophets, pastors, teachers, evangelists, and so forth.

7. We believe in the gift of tongues, prophecy, revelation, visions, healing, interpretation of tongues, and so forth.

8. We believe the Bible to be the word of God as far as it is translated correctly; we also believe the Book of Mormon to be the word of God.

9. We believe all that God has revealed, all that He does now reveal, and we believe that He will yet reveal many great and important things pertaining to the Kingdom of God.

10. We believe in the literal gathering of Israel and in the restoration of the Ten Tribes; that Zion (the New Jerusalem) will be built upon the American continent; that Christ will reign personally upon the earth; and, that the earth will be renewed and receive its paradisiacal glory.

11. We claim the privilege of worshiping Almighty God according to the dictates of our own conscience, and allow all men the same privilege, let them worship how, where, or what they may.

12. We believe in being subject to kings, presidents, rulers, and magistrates, in obeying, honoring, and sustaining the law.

13. We believe in being honest, true, chaste, benevolent, virtuous, and in doing good to all men; indeed, we may say that we follow the admonition of Paul—We believe all things, we hope all things, we have endured many things, and hope to be able to endure all things. If there is anything virtuous, lovely, or of good report or praiseworthy, we seek after these things.

PRESIDENTS OF

Joseph Smith
born: Dec. 23, 1805
Sharon, VT
president: 1830-44

Brigham Young
born: June 1, 1801
Whitingham, VT
president: 1847-77

Joseph F. Smith
born: Nov. 13, 1838
Far West, MO
president: 1901-18

Heber J. Grant
born: Nov. 22, 1856
Salt Lake City, UT
president: 1918-45

George A. Smith
born: April 4, 1850
Salt Lake City, UT
president: 1945-51

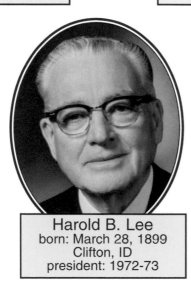

Harold B. Lee
born: March 28, 1899
Clifton, ID
president: 1972-73

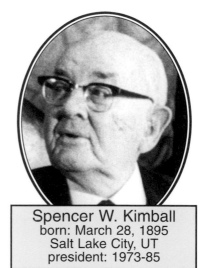

Spencer W. Kimball
born: March 28, 1895
Salt Lake City, UT
president: 1973-85

THE CHURCH

John Taylor
born: Nov. 1, 1808
Milnthorp, England
president: 1880-87

Wilford Woodruff
born: March 1, 1807
Farmington, CT
president: 1889-98

Lorenzo Snow
born: April 3, 1814
Mantua, OH
president: 1898-1901

David O. McKay
born: Sept. 8, 1873
Huntsville, UT
president: 1951-70

Joseph Fielding Smith
born: July 19, 1876
Salt Lake City
president: 1970-72

Ezra Taft Benson
born: August 4, 1899
Whitney, ID
president: 1985-94

Howard W. Hunter
born: Nov. 14, 1907
Boise, ID
president: 1994-95

Gordon B. Hinckley
born: June 23, 1910
Salt Lake City, UT
president: 1995-

MORMONS BY THE NUMBERS

Membership: April, 1830— 6[1]

Church Membership: 2005—12 million[2]

United States	5.2 million[1]
Canada	158,000[1]
Mexico	885,000[1]
Caribbean	115,000[1]
Central America	472,000[1]
South America	2.5 million[1]
Europe	412,000[1]
Asia	750,000[1]
Africa	153,000[1]
South Pacific	365,000[1]
Percentage of Mormons who are women	53[2]
Percentage of Mormons who are men	47[2]
Percentage of world's Mormons living in Utah	12[3]
Percent of Utahns who are Mormon	75[3]
Percent of Americans who are Mormon	1-2[3]
Percentage of Mormons who are Americans	48[2]
Population ranking among U.S. religions	4th[3]
Ranking among world's Christian religions	6th[3]
Full-time missionaries	60,000[4]
Average converts per day	800[4]
Average converts per year	300,000[4]
Worldwide wards and/or branches	26,237[2]
Copies of the Book of Mormon published since 1830	120,000,000[2]
Copies of the Book of Mormons distributed in 2003	4,600,000[2]
Book of Mormon—languages in print	120[2]
Number of Mormons imprisoned for polygamy in the 1880s	1,035[8]
Number of Mormons predicted by 2080	265 million[9]

UTAH BY THE NUMBERS

Utah is a demographer's dream. The high concentration of Mormons in the state—about 75%—makes it easy to track the effects of the Mormon lifestyle on health, longevity and local social trends.

Total population .... 2.2 million[5]

Mormon percentage of state population .... 75[3]

Religious denominations represented .... 67[3]

Churches, chaples, and meeting houses .... Over 1,000[3]

Percentage of state legislators who are Mormon .... 90%[6]

Ranked 1st in average family size .... 3.57 persons per family[5]

Ranked 1st for family households .... 76%[5]

Ranked 1st for the number of married-couple families .... 63%[5]

Ranked 1st for the youngest population .... 36% less than 20 years old[5]

Ranked 1st for the lowest median age .... 27 years of age[5]

Ranked 4th for number of people 25+ with a high school degree .... 91%[3]

Ranked 11th for the lowest unemployment rate .... 6.1%[5]

Fewest number of work days missed .... less than 3 per month[3]

Ranked 7th for lowest violent crime rate .... 237 cases per 100,000 persons[3]

Ranking in charitable donations .... 1st place[3]

Overall health in 2000 .... 3rd place[3]

Ranked 1st for the lowest prevalence of smoking .... 14%[3]

Ranked 1st for the lowest risk of heart disease .... 20% below national average[3]

Ranked 1st for the lowest number of cancer cases .... 239.5 cases per 100,000 people[3]

Ranked 3rd for average lifetime .... 78 years of age[7]

Ranked 2nd for the lowest overall death rate .... 5.6 deaths per 1,000[3]

Ranked 1st for fertility rate .... 2.75 births per woman[5]

4th fastest growth rate .... 30% (national average is 13.2%)[3]

Percentage of Utah households that predominantly speak English .... 88[5]

Percentage of Utah households that predominantly speak Spanish .... 7[5]

Percentage of Utah households that predominantly speak other Indo European languages .... 3[5]

Percentage of Utah households that predominantly speak Asian and Pacific Island languages .... 2[5]

C H U R C H

December 23, 1805 — Joseph Smith born to Joseph and Lucy Mack Smith in Sharon, VT

Spring, 1820 — Smith receives his First Vision, a visit from God and Jesus Christ

September, 1823 — Angel Moroni visits Smith and tells him of ancient gold plates

September, 1827 — Smith receives gold plates at Hill Cumorah, near Palmyra, NY

Spring, 1830 — The Book of Mormon is published; Church founded in upstate New York

1831-38 — Church relocates to Kirtland, OH; first temple dedicated in 1836

February, 1835 — Twelve apostles chosen and first Quorum of the Seventy organized

August, 1835 — First edition of the Doctrine and Covenants published

July, 1837 — First missionaries arrive in England, led by Heber C. Kimball

July, 1838 — Church relocates to Independence, MO, future site for the City of Zion

October 27, 1838 — Missouri Gov. Boggs issues "extermination order," expelling Mormons from state

October 30, 1838 — Hauns Mill Massacre; 18 murdered by Missouri militia

December, 1838 — Smith and other church leaders imprisoned in Liberty Jail

Winter, 1839 — Led by Brigham Young, 10,000-plus Mormons flee Missouri for Illinois

Spring, 1839 — Smith freed from jail; Nauvoo, Illinois settled by Mormons

Spring, 1842 — Relief Society organized

July, 1843 — Smith receives revelation on polygamy

January, 1844 — Smith declares his candidacy for U.S. President

June, 1844 — anti-Mormon *Nauvoo Expositor* destroyed on Smith's orders

June, 1844 — Smith arrested; mob storms Carthage Jail and murders him

February, 1846 — Mormons begin exodus west

September 12, 1846 — Battle of Nauvoo; remaining Mormons driven out of Illinois

July 24, 1847 — Young enters the Salt Lake Valley and declares, "This is the right place."

October, 1848 — Nauvoo Temple burns to the ground due to repeated arson and a tornado

1849 — Perpetual Emigrating Fund established; helps 26,000 emigrants reach Utah

1850 — England boasts more church members (30,000) than the U.S. (26,000)

June, 1850 — *Deseret News* published as first newspaper in Utah Territory

September, 1850 — Brigham Young appointed governor of Utah Territory

August, 1852 — Plural marriage publicly announced

1853 — Construction of the Salt Lake Temple begins

1856-60 — Handcart system brings thousands of emigrants to Utah

Utah Historical Society

*Joseph Smith, leading
the Nauvoo Legion*

TIMELINE

September, 1857 — Mountain Meadows Massacre in southern Utah; 120 emigrants killed

1857-58 — The Utah War

October, 1861 — Transcontinental telegraph joined near Salt Lake City

1866 — George Q. Cannon and Sons established (later Deseret Book)

October, 1867 — First General Conference held at new Salt Lake Tabernacle

March, 1869 — Church-owned ZCMI opens; first department store in the U.S.

May, 1869 — Golden Spike driven; Transcontinental Railroad completed at Promontory, UT

January 1, 1870 — First edition of *Mormon Tribune* (later *The Salt Lake Tribune*)

February, 1870 — Utah Territorial legislature gives women the vote

October, 1875 — Salt Lake Tabernacle dedicated; Brigham Young Academy founded (later BYU)

August 29, 1877 — Brigham Young dies

October, 1880 — John Taylor succeeds Young; The Pearl of Great Price accepted as scripture

1882-90 — 1,035 Utahns imprisoned for polygamy

February, 1885 — Taylor and other church leaders go into hiding

September, 1890 — President Woodruff issues "The Manifesto," outlawing Mormon polygamy

April, 1893 — Salt Lake Temple dedicated after 40 years of construction

November, 1894 – Genealogical Society of Utah organized

January 4, 1896 — Utah becomes 45th state

1900 — Worldwide Mormon population is approximately 283,000

Autumn, 1912 — First seminary program opens at Granite High School in Salt Lake City

July, 1929 — Mormon Tabernacle Choir begins weekly, national radio broadcasts

April, 1936 — Church Security (later "Welfare") Program introduced

1947 — Membership of the LDS Church reaches 1 million

1955 — First Mormon temple outside North America is dedicated in Zurich, Switzerland

1964 — Church membership surpasses 2 million

1965 — Family Home Evening program formally inaugurated

March, 1978 — President Spencer Kimball receives revelation granting blacks the priesthood

1980 — Church membership surpasses 4 million

1990 — Church membership surpasses 7 million

2000 — President Gordon B. Hinckley announces 100th Mormon temple

April, 2000 — Conference Center completed in Salt Lake City

The Salt Lake Tribune

*The
"Lion of the Lord"
Brigham Young*

DESTINATIONS

Hill Cumorah is where Joseph Smith discovered the gold plates. The visitors' center highlights the founding of the church as well as Book of Mormon history. *603 State Rt. 21, Palmyra, NY 14522. (312) 597-5851.*

Historic Kirtland includes a museum and visitors' center, a historic village with restored homes and shops, and the first Mormon temple. *Visitors' center: 7800 Kirtland-Chardon Rd., Kirtland, OH 44094. (440) 256-9805.*

Independence, Missouri gives one the opportunity to learn more about Missouri's importance to Mormons and the church's history here. *Visitors' center: 937 W. Walnut St., Independence, MO 64051. (816) 836-3466.*

Liberty Jail Historic Site has been restored to honor Joseph Smith and five other church leaders who were imprisoned here. *216 N. Main, Liberty, MO 64068. (816) 781-3188.*

Nauvoo, Illinois is home to a wealth of historic sites celebrating the Mormons' time in Illinois, including the reconstructed Nauvoo Temple. *Visitors' center: Main and Young St., Nauvoo, IL 62345. 1-888-453-6434.*

Carthage Jail has been restored as a monument to Joseph and Hyrum Smith, who were martyred here on June 27, 1844. *307 Walnut St., Carthage, IL 62321. (217) 357-2989.*

Mormon Trail Center at Historic Winter Quarters offers one a glimpse into the hardships the pioneers suffered— and the determination that saved them— in their trek west. *3215 State St., Omaha, NE 69112. (402) 453-9372.*

This Is The Place Historic Park celebrates the pioneers' arrival in the Salt Lake Valley, featuring a living history museum and Old Deseret Village. *2601 Sunnyside Ave., Salt Lake City, UT 84108. (801) 582-1847.*

Temple Square is the heart of the Mormon Church. It includes the Salt Lake Temple, Tabernacle, Assembly Hall, Family Search Center, and two visitors' centers. *50 W. North Temple, Salt Lake City, UT 84150. 1-800-537-9703.*

The Beehive House has been fully restored and is open for visitors to see where Brigham Young lived as president of the Mormon Church and governor of the Utah Territory. *67 E. South Temple, Salt Lake City, UT 84111. (801) 240-2671.*

The Conference Center is the newest addition to the Temple Square area and the largest religious structure in the Americas. *60 W. North Temple, Salt Lake City, UT 84150. (801) 240-0075.*

Museum of Church History and Art features fine works of art and interactive exhibits that bring the church's history to life, including an original 1830 Book of Mormon. *45 N. West Temple, Salt Lake City, UT 84150. (801) 240-4615.*

Family History Library allows one to freely browse the largest genealogical data base in the world, with over 2 billion names. *35 N. West Temple, Salt Lake City, UT 84150. (801) 240-2331.*

St. George has several historic sites: the St. George Temple, Tabernacle, and Brigham Young's Winter Home, a museum dedicated to the pioneer. *St. George Area Visitors' Bureau: 1835 Convention Center Dr., St. George, UT 84755. 1-800-634-5747.*

MORMON PAGEANTS

Arizona Easter Pageant: Jesus the Christ, April, Mesa, AZ. (480) 964-7164.
Castle Valley Pageant, July/August, Castle Dale, UT. (435) 381-2362.
City of Joseph Pageant, July/August, Nauvoo, IL. 1-800-453-0022.
Clarkston Pageant—Martin Harris: The Man Who Knew, August, Clarkston, UT. (435) 563-0059.
Hill Cumorah Pageant: America's Witness for Christ, July, Palmyra, NY. (585) 248-9135.
Mormon Miracle Pageant, June, Manti, UT. 1-888-255-8860.
Oakland Temple Pageant, July, Oakland, CA. (510) 531-1475.

For more Mormon-related tourism information, visit www.lds.org/placestovisit

MORMONISM ON THE WEB

Church Sponsored
www.lds.org — The official web site of The Church of Jesus Christ of Latter-day Saints
www.mormon.org — An introduction to the Mormon Church and its basic beliefs
www.scriptures.lds.org — Access complete texts of Mormon scriptures
www.Newsroom.lds.org — Statistics, press releases, photos, and selected articles
www.VisitTempleSquare.com — Tourist information for Temple Square, Salt Lake City
www.FamilySearch.org — Access the church's vast genealogical database
www.MormonTabernacleChoir.org — Information, history and schedules for the choir

General Mormon Interest
www.lds-mormon.com — Mormonism and the LDS Church
www.byu.edu — Official web site for Brigham Young University
www.farms.byu.edu — BYU's Foundation for Ancient Research and Mormon Studies
www.zionsbest.com — Mormon books, articles and papers
www.lds.org/placestovisit — Browse various Mormon tourist sites
www.nauvoo.com — Historical and tourist information on Nauvoo, IL
www.MormonTrail.net — History of the Mormon Trail
www.handcart.com — History of handcart migration
www.HistoryToGo.utah.gov — Includes history of early Mormon settlements in Utah
www.DeseretBook.com — A Utah-based book dealer specializing in Mormon texts
www.SamWellers.com — Salt Lake book store specializing in rare Mormon books
www.KenSandersBooks.com — Salt Lake book store featuring Mormon-related books

Mormonism and Mormon Lifestyle
www.ProvidentLiving.org — Church sponsored, offering temporal guidance
www.LDSliving.com — Mormon lifestyle, magazines, books, and more
www.MeridianMagazine.com — Mormon lifestyle and current events
www.MormonsToday.com — Current events with a Mormon perspective
www.LDSfilm.com — A guide to Mormon-related and Mormon-produced cinema
www.FamousMormons.net — A very current guide to Mormon celebrities
www.LDSsingles.com — Mormon dating service
www.LDSmingle.com — Mormon dating service
www.SingleSaints.com — Lifestyle site for single Mormons

General Religious Information
www.ReligiousResources.org — A directory of religious resources on the web
www.adherents.com — A collection of statistics and religious geography citations
www.irr.org — Institute for Religious Research
www.carm.org — Christian Apologetics & Research Ministry

RECOMMENDED BOOKS

Scripture

The Book of Mormon (Deseret Book)
The Doctrine and Covenants (Deseret Book)
The Pearl of Great Price (Deseret Book)
The Bible

Doctrine

Are Mormons Christians?, Stephen E. Robinson (Bookcraft, 1991)
Believing Christ: The Parable of Bicy, Stephen E. Robinson (Deseret Book, 1992)
The Great Apostacy, James E. Talmage (Deseret Book, 1909)
In the Footsteps of Lehi, Warren and Michael Aston (Deseret Book, 1994)
Jesus the Christ: A Study of the Messiah and His Mission, James E. Talmage (Deseret Book, 1906)
Mormon Doctrine, Bruce McConkie (Deseret Book, 1966)

History

500 Little Known Facts About Mormonism, George W. Givens (Bonneville Books, 2002)
Early Mormonism and the Magic World View, D. Michael Quinn (Signature Books, 1998)
The Gathering of Zion: The Story of the Mormon Trail, Wallace Stegner (McGraw, 1964)
Joseph Smith: The First Mormon, Donna Hill (Signature Books, 1977)
The Mormon Experience: A History of the Latter-day Saints, Arrington (Univ. of Illinois Press, 1992)
Mormon Polygamy: A History, Richard S. Van Wagoner (Signature Books, 1986)
Mormon Trail, Yesterday and Today, William E. Hill (Oregon-California Trails Assoc.)
Twelve Mormon Homes, Elizabeth W. Kane (Signature Books, 1875)

Mormon Life

America's Choir: A Commemorative Portrait of the Mormon Tabernacle Choir, Heidi Swinton (Deseret, 2004)
I Walked To Zion: True Stories of Young Pioneers on the Mormon Trail, Susan A. Madsen (Deseret, 1994)
Lighten Up!. Chieko Okazaki (Deseret, 1992)

Also available from White Horse Books

Dinosaurs of Utah
I Spy A Nephite
Kirby Soup for the Soul
J. Golden Kimball Stories
More J. Golden Kimball Stories
This Is The Place
Welcome To Utah

William Clayton composed "Come, Come, Ye Saints" in tribute to those that made the trek West. Clayton himself was among the first pioneers to enter the Salt Lake Valley. His song has become the Mormon anthem.

Come, Come, Ye Saints

W. Clayton

1. Come, come, ye Saints, no toil nor labor fear, But with joy wend your way;
2. Why should we mourn, or think our lot is hard? 'Tis not so; all is right!
3. We'll find the place which God for us prepared, Far a-way in the West;
4. And should we die before our journey's through, Hap-py day! all is well!

Tho' hard to you this jour-ney may appear, Grace shall be as your day.
Why should we think to earn a great re-ward, If we now shun the fight?
Where none shall come to hurt or make a-fraid; There the Saints will be blessed.
We then are free from toil and sor-row too; With the just we shall dwell.

'Tis bet-ter far for us to strive Our use-less cares from
Gird up your loins, fresh cour-age take, Our God will nev-er
We'll make the air with mu-sic ring — Shout prais-es to our
But if our lives are spared a-gain To see the Saints, their

us to drive; Do this, and joy your hearts will swell — All is well! All is well!
us for-sake; And soon we'll have this truth to tell — All is well! All is well!
God and King; A-bove the rest these words we'll tell — All is well! All is well!
rest ob-tain, O how we'll make this cho-rus swell — All is well! All is well!

BIBLIOGRAPHY

"2000 Census," U.S. Census Bureau, www.census.gov

Berrett, William E., The Restored Church. Salt Lake City: Deseret Book, 1965.

Church of Jesus Christ of Latter-day Saints, www.lds.org, www.newsroom.lds.org, www.scriptures.lds.org, www.lds.org/placestovisit, www.lds.org/temples

Fidel, Steve, "Salt Lake Plugged in to the Internet." Newsweek, 1998.

"Sampling of Latter-day Saint/Utah Demographics and Social Statistics from National Sources," www.adherents.com

Sheler, Jeffery L., "The Mormon Moment: The Church of Jesus Christ of Latter-day Saints Grows by Leaps and Bounds." U.S. New & World Report, November 11, 1998.

Slaughter, William and Patrick Bagley, Church History Timeline. Salt Lake City: Deseret Book, 1996.

Stegner, Wallace, Mormon Country. New York: Bonanza Books, 1942.

Van Biema, David, "Kingdom Come." Time Magazine, August 4, 1997.

Utah Historical Society, www.historytogo.utah.gov

"Mormons By The Numbers / Utah By The Numbers" Sources

1 – BBC: Religion & Ethics, www.bbc.co.uk

2 – Church of Jesus Christ of Latter-day Saints, www.newsroom.lds.org

3 – "Sampling of Latter-day Saint/Utah Demographics and Social Statistics from National Sources," www.adherents.com

4 – Christian Apologetics Research Ministry, www.carm.org/lds/ldsstatistics

5 – "2000 Census," U.S. Census Bureau, www.census.gov

6 – O'Driscoll, Patrick. "Prosecuting Polygamists." USA Today, May 14, 2001.

7 – Utah Governor's Office, http://governor.utah.gov/dea/Rankings/States/lifetimegh.htm

8 – Slaughter, William and Patrick Bagley, Church History Timeline. Salt Lake City: Deseret Book, 1996.

9 – Sheler, Jeffery L., "The Mormon Moment: The Church of Jesus Christ of Latter-day Saints Grows by Leaps and Bounds." U.S. New & World Report, November 11, 1998.

Photo Credits and Sources

Church Archives, The Church of Jesus Christ of Latter-day Saints

The Salt Lake Tribune

Utah Historical Society

www.lds.org